cra-que-lure

poems by

Elizeya Quate

Finishing Line Press
Georgetown, Kentucky

cra-que-lure

ACKNOWLEDGMENTS

The poems "What's Real Is Feeling Opposite" and "Obvious Concealments"
appeared in *Work to a calm* and in *Killer Whale Journal* (Vol.5) alongside
"Sickness" ("This Perforated Morning") in 2016.
"You" and "Flying" appeared *e-ratio journal* (Vol.23) in 2017.
"What's Real Is Feeling In-Between" appeared in *Bonk! Magazine* (UK) in
2017.
"What's Real is Feeling Opposite", "Obvious Concealments", "Night River"
and "Flying", also appeared in *Spam Zine* in 2017.
"What's Real Is Feeling The Same" ("real things we never did") and "Make a
Living Grow Up No You Don't Want That" appeared printed in *Hollow: Issue
V* published by Broken Tooth Press in 2017.

Megathanks to Lisa Galloway & Ralph Paone for offering the key reacts, Kat
Culture for being an amazing collaborator who always sees the lines within
the lines & to my oddlovely comrades at Schema & The Castro Writer's
Cooperative. ❦

Publisher: Leah Maines
Editor: Christen Kincaid
Cover Art: Katie Williams
Author Photo: Lucia Moore
Cover Design: Elizabeth Maines McCleavy

Printed in the USA on acid-free paper.
Order online: www.finishinglinepress.com

Author inquiries and mail orders:
Finishing Line Press
P. O. Box 1626
Georgetown, Kentucky 40324
U. S. A.

Table of Contents

**cra-
que-
lure**

*slender
little
heart-
crack
poems*

What's Real Is Feeling Opposite

None of
this is real.
I am
a bus station.
You are
a pair of
enormous
sunglasses.
I am
a motel lobby.
You are
a road
sign war-
ning of
mudslides.
I am
a steering
wheel.
You are
a Bible Belt
radio station.
I am
an empty
intersection.
You are
the horizon
of I-80,
flush
-ing
scar-
let
with
to-
morrow's
dawn.

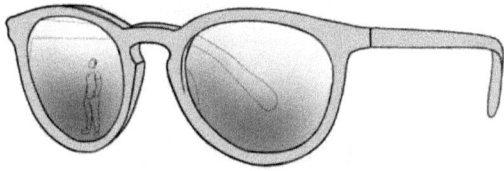

Obvious Concealments

Sometimes
I want to
conceal
that sweet
lemon
glimpse of
last sum-
mer's moon
inside this
poem.
That's
not what
I'm try-
ing to
do here,
though.
At least
I'm not
trying
very hard.
Obvious
conceal-
ments
aren't
really
conceal-
ments, I
think, be-
cause they
only
draw at-
tention
to what
we're not

supposed
to wish
was even
there.

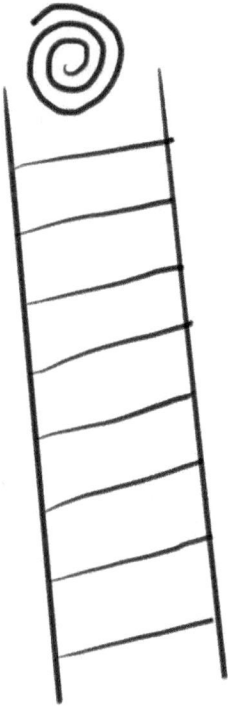

Bright River

Today
what my
closed
eyes
con-
ceal: a
quiver
of moon-
beams a-
cross your
drip-
ping
breasts.
Above
the whis-
per of
bull-
rushes,
our fing-
ers stretch
towards
the
shape
of
all
our
body's
un-
asked
quest-
ions,
and re-
turn,

in-
flamed &
still,
un-

satisfied.

A Poem That Makes More Poems Like Itself

This poem
makes more
poems like
itself (I hope).
But maybe
we'll find out.
(Together!?)

Some poems
Are like
STDs, ex-
cept they'd
be STPs
(P for poem).
Sexually
Transmitted
Poems.

Poems like
the love that
keeps on
loving,
the love that
makes more
love over time.

Un-
fortunately,
to-
day
my
mind
is
fresh

out of
that partic-
ular poem.
So   I wrote
this odd, mislabeled one in-

stead.

Questions

I start to
remember
all the
questions
that you
left me
with,
staring at
our future
through
the fiss-
ures
of my
hands,
doubting
everything.
Then I
start to
forget
all the
questions
that you
left me
with,
staring at
our past,
through
the fiss-
ures
of my
hands,
saving

nothing

Heat-poem, Moody Aubade

What you
once gave
to me
was the
feeling for
a certain
time of day.

Right before
dawn when
our fevers
clung to-
gether, lay-
ing in a
dirty bed
our eyes
would
open, sud-
denly a-
flame
against
the dark-
ness.

Then
staring
up our
breath
would
hold
and
rush
in
bouts
of
care-
ful
sym-
metry,
as we
won-
dered
if
the other
won-
dered
if
the
other

was really even there.

Getting Dressed

First I'm
naked.
That's no
good
so I
put on
a sock,
just
one
holey
sock
I saw
it lying
on
the
mattress.

Now I'm
less
naked
but still
not non-
naked
enough
to go
outside,
to be
in public.
I find
a dress,
a chemise,
a fez,
some blue
scarves,
I go into
the kitchen &
put on some
tongs,
a pot, a ladle
around my head.

Then you
come
in wearing
your sun-
glasses
and pull
it all off
be-
cause
you say
that if
I stay
one

more mo-
ment
in
such
wrong
clothes
you
just
might
die.

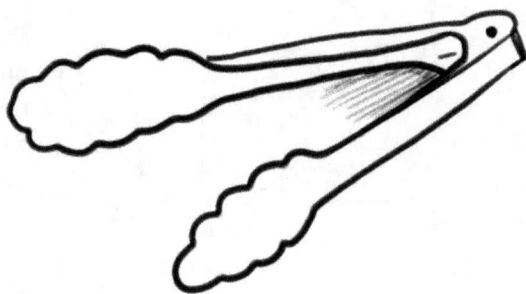

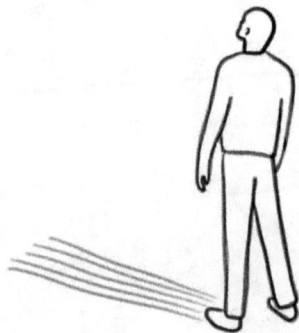

This Chapbook, Craquelure

This chapbook was
originally
a novel
called "Title"
about two
entirely
fictitious
heterosexual,
white lovers
from middle-
class back-
grounds named
"Name!"
and "Girl?"

They
fall in love.

It's difficult-
ish, but
then every-
thing works
itself
out in the
end.

Hurray.

It's good,
I think,
for things
like that
stupid
kind of
chapbook

to simply
not work

out.

Skull/Thighs

You plop
down on
the matt-
ress, grab
me by
my bangs
and shove
my head
down
in between
your naked
thighs.
Then
you squee-
ze (until
it's
like
my
skull
is
pop-
ping!)

I
lick
and
slurp
while
you
squee-
ze my
slkull
(pop-pop!)
O-
dor or
camphor,
now some-
thing
fer-
al; rainy
fur; I
fee; frag-
ile, I
feel float-
ing, I
feel swoon-
ed by

by the gooey shelter of your thighs.

Geisting

I'd
have
to be
a real
sucker
to con-
fess any
pass-
ion for for-
ever-
ness.
Eternity
has
now be-
come
to seem so
untimely,
a
yester
year's
wrong
chord.

Only
lov-
e that
rots and
spoils,
that's
us
now, (sup-
-posedly).

Drift be-
comes
our fix-
ed idea,

our
core pre-
occupation.

Today
what my
closed
eyes
conceal:
a
small
eyes
conceal:
a
small
boat,
its
wake
purl-
ing
be-
neath
the
arches
of
our
bare
feet,
as
it
goes
slid-
ing
a-
way
from
the

edge
of
last
sum-
mer's
heat-
poem.

Behind
closed
eyes,
I re-
member
thinking:
nothing,
as our
last
moorings
finally
come
undone.

Eating

Food's be-
come a
place to
put more
gray into,
like all
the hours
we left
lingering
at the
door-
ways
to each
other's
stormy
declarations.

My eyes
go fool-
ing a-
round
with a
plate's
edge,
a loop of
grease-
bound
sun, & then
go dull
again, sigh.

Night
has fall-
en, food's
turned
cold. Back
to the micro-
wave.

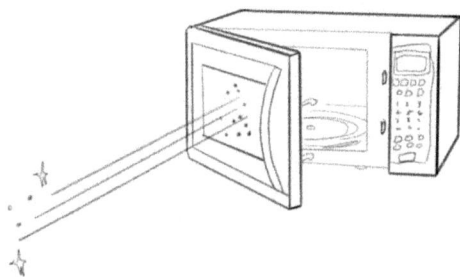

A Promise to Break

What I'm
asking is
for you
to break
me AGAIN,
break me
all the way OPEN.

> (I don't care
> if it hurts)
> as long as
> you promise
> that you'll
> keep break-
> ing me, OVER
> and OVER.

Sadly, even
a promise
to break
was not
the kind
of prom-
ise you
knew how
to KEEP.

What's Real Is Feeling In-Between

None of
this is real.
I spent to-
day wishing
for the words
I wanted
but never
had using
the words
I had but
never wanted,
until the
burnt sky
revealed
what's not
our careful
symmetry.

What I do when I feel you feeling my aching
isn't madness, not exactly—there's still too much
stupid wishfulness cleaving to my treacherous
memory, the way a fray of paper poses the endless
child's question: *why?*

What I do when I write you writing my aching
isn't longing, not exactly—there's still too much
left unsaid that's trapped behind the blinking
cursors of the days before I could even breathe to
write your name.

What I do when I think you thinking my aching
isn't daydreaming, not exactly—there's still too
many teeth catching my mind's rough edges,
precipices where I ought not linger (even when I
cannot help but linger) even now.

None of
this is real.
Out from
each
slender
little
heart-
crack,
our
scar-
let
dawns
will
fade
until
our care-
ful sy-
mmetry di
  ssolves

23

Sleeping

Sleep
comes
the
same
way
I do,
thick
and
ghostly
after a
brief, one-
hand-
ed struggle.
To-
night
our
ghosts
go
out
wand-
ering
&
alone
here
I am
still
much
much
too
tired
for
any
sort
of
sleep.

You

It has
taken
me long
enough
to recog-
nize that
you're
the state
I'm al-
ways in
after wine
has turn-
ed my
lips the
co-
balt blue
of this
& every
even-
ing's
lone-
liness.

Make A Living Grow Up No You Don't Want That

in homage to kathy acker and dj khaled

stupid kid you're just like me now
look what you've gone and done

nasty kid you're just like colors
you're full of yourself you're ruined

strange kid you've gone too far now
you've gone & become too many poems

weird kid you could do yourself a favor by
staying away from yourself for your whole life

bad kid you know in the end your itches
won't stay put they'll wreck your body

evil kid you're so undead now just like me
so tell us what bright poems will you become?

Night River

Be-
side the
banks
of the Po-
tomac my
tongue
extends
to caress
the glow-
ing pink
of
your
nipples,
as the
loops of
moonwater
lick &
shish
around
the
supple
roots
of all
these other-
worldly
trees.

Sickness

This morning
I look at
with one
eye stares
back with
100,000.
I can't
tell if
it's filled
with tiny
holes or
not, my
stomach aches.

On the
subway
I fell into
a man.
I said
I was
sorry.
I don't
know
if I
was
sorry, I
don't
know
if he
accepted
my ap-
ology.
He didn't
have any
hair but
I think
we were

about
the same
age. That
got me
thinking.

This morning
I look at
with one
eye stares   I can't tell
back with   if it's filled with tiny holes or not, my
  > zero.   stomach aches.

What's Real Is Feeling the Same

there are so many things we said we'd do

whenever

i hate talking like that, it makes me feel old

as if the evening means nothing more than blank

sleeping before another day of dread

there are so many things we said we'd do

tomorrow

i hate talking like that, it makes me feel dishonest

as if we could trace our way to the doorstep of a

phantom hero's future

there are so many things we said we'd do when we

grew up & finally felt in charge of things, in

control

see? i told you, i really do hate talking like this

all the real things we never did, they make me

feel that everyone i've ever known has

failed

Flying

A-
cross
the
sky
I'm
think-
ing
how
the
air
is
not
really
emp-
ty
up
here
at
all,
in-
stead
the
air
is
full
of
tiny
hands
we
can-
not
see.

Craquelure

noun, plural craquelures
[krak-loo rz, krak-loo rz; French krakuh-lyr]

a network of fine cracks or crackles on the surface of a painting, caused chiefly by shrinkage of paint film or varnish.

When you were writing these poems, remember how you felt deep down? Remember how half-sheepishly you wanted to cry when the person you were in love with told you that your togetherness was over? How the aftermath of that moment felt both inexorable and also impossible? How you fell into a suede oblivion & hid all these slender little cracks deep beneath the shrinking surface of every endless day? How even though you knew that such heartbreak feelings are extremely clichéd and/or inevitably cringeworthy to write about, that nothing about this knowledge allowed you to stop feeling so heartbroken?

Since that maudlin period of these poems' composition, several half-ok thoughts have been suggested to you by shrewder associates:
- Be grateful for what you have
- Ephemeral intensities are still worthwhile, and truly, doesn't everything good in life one day come to an end?
- The future is (mostly) unknowable
- Depression is a somatic form of arrogance: it's your body convincing you that you can know tomorrow will be worse. The truth is: you cannot know. Chaos & unknowability offer the best evidence-based negation of pessimism.

So just please keep doing the simple
things: go to sleep, make some coffee,
write a poem, go for a walk, gaze at
the sky, take a deep breath & then do it
all over again. Keeping one's minor
habits in practice is the surest path
towards one's liveableness & perhaps
a plural self worthy of a plural
other's love & care.

Elizeya Quate is the nom of Edmund Zagorin, a writer and performer based in the Bay Area. Raised in Tenleytown DC, Quate's first book *The Face of Our Town* (KERNPUNKT Press, 2016) is a fun series of interconnected stories about the serious fun of interconnectedness. In December 2016, *The Face of Our Town* Kindle ebook achieved #1 Amazon Bestseller status in the category of Popular Culture: Antiques & Collectibles, and #8 Bestseller in the category of Short Story Collections. Quate's publications include a nomination for *Year's Best Weird Fiction Vol. 3* ("Peru, Illinois" in Axolotl, 2015), *Ground Fresh Thursday, E-ratio, Big Lucks, Killer Whale, Intrinsick Magazine, Sparkle + Blink, Work to a calm, Maudlin House, Sleepingfish, Tahoma Literary Review, Minor Literatures, 3Elements Review, Chicago Literati, Two Cities Review, Joyland Michigan Writer's Series, The American Prospect, The Huffington Post, Critical Moment* and the anthology *Writing That Risks: New Work From Beyond The Mainstream* (Redbridge Press, 2013). Quate has read at Quiet Lightning, Perfectly Queer, Inside StoryTime, tNY Pre-AWP Showcase and has performed versions of Seminar on Autosophy at Think Tank Gallery, Adobe Books, The Convent, The Last Bookstore and the Pataphysical Research and Metachanics Union. Quate writes book reviews for *The Los Angeles Review*, and has made interactive talk/art for The Gallery Project, Start Gallery, Zajia Lab, Come Out & Play Festival and Odd Salon.

Katie Williams (Kat) is a multimedia artist dabbling in illustration, painting, performance, singing/songwriting, and improv for acts of radical play, colorful abstractions, and resistance. Kat also performs at times under the stage name Kat Culture. She currently resides in California and is always down to collaborate with other artists who share mutual interests (say hi!). www.katculture.com.